Young
George Washington
America's First President

A Troll First-Start® Biography

by Andrew Woods
illustrated by John Himmelman

Troll Associates

Library of Congress Cataloging-in-Publication Data

Woods, Andrew.
    Young George Washington: America's first president / by Andrew
Woods; illustrated by John Himmelman.
        p.   cm.—(First-start biographies)
    Summary: A simple biography of the man who was in charge of
America's army during the Revolution and became the new nation's
first president.
    ISBN 0-8167-2540-3 (lib. bdg.)   ISBN 0-8167-2541-1 (pbk.)
    1. Washington, George, 1732-1799—Juvenile literature.
2. Presidents—United States—Biography—Juvenile literature.
[1. Washington, George, 1732-1799.   2. Presidents.]   I. Himmelman,
John, ill.   II. Title.   III. Series.
E332.79.W66   1992
973.4'1'092—dc20
[B]   91-26405

This edition published in 2002.

20   19   18   17   16   15   14   13

George Washington was America's
first president.

He was born in Virginia in 1732.
In those days America was ruled
by the king of Great Britain.
Virginia was a British colony.

Young George didn't care who ruled
America. He was too busy playing
games and helping his family on
their farm.

When George was 7, he started school.
He went to a one-room schoolhouse.
Children of all ages sat together
and were taught by one teacher.

When George was 11, a very sad thing
happened. His father died. George was
sent to stay with his older brother
Lawrence.

Lawrence lived on a big farm called
Mount Vernon. George loved it there.

At Mount Vernon, George learned
a lot about farming. But there was
time for fun, too. He hunted, fished,
and rode horses. George loved riding
horses most of all.

When George got older, he joined
Virginia's army. He led many attacks
against the French and Indians.

George was a good leader.
Soon he became the head
of Virginia's army.

One day George met Martha Custis.
She was a young widow with two
children. George and Martha fell
in love. Soon they were married.

George took his new family to live
at Mount Vernon. They were very
happy there.

But life in America was not easy.
The British king made the American
colonies pay high taxes. And he passed
laws the people did not like.

18

George Washington wanted to fight
for America's freedom. Many people
agreed with him.

The colonists went to war against
Great Britain. This war was called
the American Revolution.

Washington was in charge of the
whole American army. The army
fought hard against the British.

Washington's men had little money or supplies. But Washington was a brave leader. He made his army believe it could win.

Finally, after 8 long years, the
war ended. The colonies were free.
America was free!

After the Revolution, Washington still
had important jobs to do. He helped
create the Constitution. People set
down rules for the new government
to follow.

Then he was chosen to be the first
president of the United States.
He was president for 8 years.

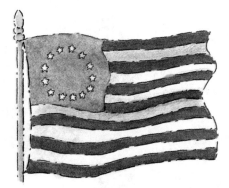

When his days as president were over,
Washington and his wife went home to
Mount Vernon. Two years later,
George Washington died there.

Across the river from Mount Vernon is
Washington, D.C., the nation's capital.
It was named in Washington's honor.

America has had many presidents.
But few are as well-loved as
George Washington.

Index